What
Is
Fair

poems

JAMES
HARMON
CLINTON

Louisiana State University Press
Baton Rouge and London   1997

06 05 04 03 02 01 00 99 98 97   5 4 3 2 1

Designer: Michele Myatt Quinn
Typeface: Galliard
Printer and binder: Thomson-Shore, Inc.

Library of Congress Cataloging-in-Publication Data
Clinton, James Harmon, 1946–
    What is fair : poems / by James Harmon Clinton.
        p. cm.
    ISBN 0-8071-2195-9 (cloth : alk. paper). — ISBN 0-8071-2196-7
(paper : alk. paper)
    I. Title
PS3553.L5645W47   1997
811'.54—dc21   97-18676
                                                                        CIP

Some of the poems in this book appeared previously, in some cases in slightly different form, in the following publications: *Context South* ("Swept Away by a Confluence of Events"), *Cross Roads* ("Another False Spring"; "Gathering Evening"), *God's Bar: Unplugged* ("Jay's Lounge and Cockpit, 1979"), *Howling Dog* ("A Six-Pack and a Long Fuse"), *Mobius* ("Passion's Sextant"), *New Voices in Poetry and Prose* ("Paper Cut"), *Poet* ("Marcel on Fire"), *Riverrun* ("Ray's Farm, Late December"), *Sonoma Mandala* ("The Seventh Movement"), Spoon River Poetry Review ("Amanda, 1961"; "Particle Storm"), *Whisper* ("A Schedule of Trains"), and *Xavier Review* ("Black Wool, Red Satin Lining").

for Susan

CONTENTS

What
Is
Fair

The Rathe Primrose

A black rubber tube half the circumference of a fire hose,
a gridiron in length, wraps its slow curve around the infield,
around Sonny's thick torso, through his legs. Water pulses
blindly down the length of the tunnel and erupts through

the brass nozzle, the diffracting spray smothering the dust
that has been rising from the main diamond all day. Each drop
pummels the sere surface, compacting and rejuvenating
and cooling the field, setting it up like a great clay court.

Sonny concentrates on the mound, the space around each base,
the vast expanse that will later be the stage for shortstops:
dust-divers, stiflers of offense. The onset of his labors
has silenced the park, given it respite from the daylong

pickup games of scrub and pepper, the uncharted agon
patched together by the summer warriors. Sonny turns
toward third base, throws the hose over his shoulder, and drags
it from the field. He returns with a rolling bucket of lime,

commences the limning of coach's and batter's boxes
and the almost perfect vectors that show, now for later,
what is fair. Deep in one corner of the park, beyond the fence
that runs from foul ground into deepest left center field,

beyond the drainage ditch which rides the fence line, a few
freckled boys improvise a playing field strewn with pinecones
and crabgrass. Six or seven of us linger, hoping for one sweet
true swing, one sonorous intersection of ash and horsehide,

and the ensuing headlong sprint, the careening, tumbling slide
toward home, the dive to evade the catcher and the ignominy
of being out. On deck, I twist the bat until a voice dry as pine
summons me from the brink, and I go where my father calls.

The First Trains

may be dreams, toddler reveries,
or a gift from my brother, home from the war
with his big green bathtub Nash,
six feet of elbows and knees in the creases

of his uniform. He sprawls on the linoleum
floor, smiles and shows me the tinplate
locomotive, connects the track and lets the train
circle him, run through the tunnel

of his arms and legs. It is a streamliner,
it is a diesel: no, it's a steamer, flaming
down the Frisco tracks toward Hoxie
where my mother and I spend blue hours

making connections with the Missouri Pacific
train to Little Rock. From the window seat,
I can see the engine engraving the train's arc
along the White River banks, then I lose sight

of it again as the track straightens on the flat
alluvial plain. It deposits us at Union Station
in Little Rock where a few days later I watch
the switcher: a boisterous chugging toy,

articulated motion and a profusion of smoke,
back and forth all the livelong winter day,
but nothing like the one that I see each morning
outside the kitchen window in Walnut Ridge

and every time I think it will run off the tracks
and into our house so I sit in my mother's lap
to eat breakfast and watch the brakeman
connecting boxcars to my early morning dreams.

Rosetta Street

It is all a postwar movie in my head,
the jerry-built subdivision, the gravel street,
the handmade toys, the bootlegger making runs
at sunset, the white frame duplex, and the way

my father opens the front door
and swings his cardboard suitcase inside.
"We're moving to Little Rock," he says,
"I got the job." I stand behind my mother,

hide in the folds of her long navy skirt,
peek around her knees to watch his
pacing presentation. "I rented a house
on Rosetta Street, two big bedrooms,

and an extra room beyond the breezeway."
I see a street bathed in dark green,
cedar dwarves and ivy. He tells her
that it is just two blocks from the bus line.

"I will ride the bus to work every day,"
he says. He tells her about a park near
the house, about swings and slides and seesaws
and baseball fields for me: I see pine trees.

He says the house has a big front porch
with a bright blue morning glory climbing
a trellis along one corner. He drops his suitcase
on the bed. "We'll take the train," he says.

I will be frightened by the train, the steam
and the hurly-burly depot. On Rosetta Street,
we will be near my sisters, near a grade school.
My father will sell carpet until he dies; my mother

will hover over my tenderest years. Hydrangeas will flank
day lilies. At night the artillery crack of wood on leather
will be seen, then heard. There a chinaberry tree will grow
and time will pass through its branches in postcard relief.

The Year the Downtown Stores Got Air Conditioning

Brand names fell from my nine-year-old tongue
like the samples cascading from the carpet rack:
Mohawk, Bigelowe, Cabin Craft, Alexander Smith, Karastan.

I stacked and restacked the area rugs,
used them as a defensive line,
diving through their bulwarks
for first downs and touchdowns.

The department moved to new quarters,
the opposite end of the downtown block,
to be part of a home center, modern,
with air conditioning, that great southern
developer of economies,
and an escalator—don't go up the down,
don't ride the handrail, don't.

I spent my youth in carpeted fields,
random-sheared and plush,
nylon, wool, and acrylic.
Under my father's reproachful stare,
I learned the peculiar odors of carpet padding:
jute, sponge, foam. I came in from the heat
of the sticky Little Rock summer
to a world where there were no other kids,
to a place where I could never be hurt
and the only competition was my wicked imagination.

Onward, He Said

I remember his teasing voice, transposing the sounds
of my first and last names. I can hear him calling
my sister "Pest" with no effort to disguise his affection.
I can feel his bass resonating in the varnished pew
of the frame church house as I struggled to find
the harmony and hosted visions, dark and wicked,
to test God's vaunted mercy.

Summer days, he drove through rural Arkansas
to measure houses for carpet, bearing with him
sample books in forty shades of beige and his youngest son,
riding shotgun. On a winding road through a national forest,
he told me a joke that he thought dirty, a bonding thing,
I guess, but it wasn't dirty, wasn't even funny,
except for the fact that he told it and laughed so hard.

Out of touch with profanity, his attempts came out wrong,
no edge, never menacing, just clumsy and funny
malapropisms of obscenity. Not inheriting his profanity
impairment, I learned to swear in alleys, garages, locker rooms.
So effective was my tutoring that family members
considered me alien. No other among us
could utter those words with such sincerity.

I can hear him cheering me on from the sideline,
tilted against the fence past the third-base dugout,
as I stared down batters and launched my prepubescent
fastball. I cannot find his cadence; I remember no sentences,
no paragraphs, though I must have heard them, at least
as he spoke with others. I ask my sister how he sounded.
She says that they talked a lot, that he gave her advice.

Damn. Maybe he didn't know what to say to me,
the accident that closed his procreative career.
I think that he must have loved me; the crinkled Brownie

prints that show us together would have you believe
that he did. My mother says that shortly before he died,
I got out of the car ahead of them one night. They sat
briefly together in the darkness watching me walk to our door.
Then he said to her, "He's a good kid, Ione."

He helped me prepare for a speech contest, sponsored
by the Optimist Club. He spelled out the word "optimism."
"O" is for onward. He died within the year.
Onward, and he died without warning, without
notice, without telling me that I was a good kid,
so I never knew. I only knew that my mother
thought so, but my mother I could always fool.

Airborne

The window fan pulled a steady breeze
through my open window, just a screen
and a billowing gauze mainsail
between my bed and all the things

that could go wrong at night. The zoo
and the asylum were just across
Fair Park from each other. Their residents
too had open windows, but no fans to stir

the night's heavier elements to a more civil
brew. Late on sleepless summer nights,
a howling arose from the park's environs.
Perhaps the lions roared first,

but it may have been the lionhearted.
Either way, the denizens of the city's cruelest
lodgements served notice to the free citizens
that no bars could ever contain such wildness.

Amanda, 1961

She sits among the bookshelves in the partially finished
basement, stares at a novel called *Interlude at Pelican Bend*.
It is midmorning and her husband is in his long white Buick
on the road to Marinette and Sturgeon Bay.

Her children are in school or with her mother-in-law
and on this first day back at home she feels the steel frame
of the butterfly chair against her gaunt thighs, reads
page twenty-seven again and again, retraces the events

that brought her to this cold, guileless state. Born to tobacco
and bourbon, she married thoughtlessly: a way out, other cities,
other dreams. Her husband, a gaudy provider, denies their lot,
raises toasts to his deft navigation of career thermals,

but they collapse, together or apart, into drossy, alcoholic afterbirth.
She loses herself in this place where July's fair lawn gives way
to January's packed ice, the warm chatter of Indian summer
to cold betrayal. Here, the sun never penetrates enough

for her psyche to flow unhindered. Here, the neighbors talk
and what she takes for love is a brutish affair that she turns
on herself. Here, family must be imported, shipped in like
hothouse flowers, only to wring their hands and shake their heads

in pity. The pristine concussion of gin's first swallow beckons
from the kitchen above, but the post-shock-treatment
will is not sufficient for destruction. She will not drink
and she will not laugh with her children and she will not dance

with her teenage brother-in-law and make his face red
with her bawdy humor. She will just try to learn why the man
at Pelican Bend is so sad when the cola-skinned girl steps out
of her plum-colored skirt and bids him to cross the room.

Evening, Birch Lake, 1962

On northern Wisconsin logging roads,
in her father's blue Dodge, we drive our shame
into the snow-deep night. Past Indian-named
lakes, across frozen creeks, we search

for a jukebox with the frequency
to deliver us from all evil. We park the car
and trudge down the fairways of the abandoned
golf course, tobogganing the slopes and traps.

We find shelter in the hallway of an open-air
roller rink, empty through the winter.
No one interrupts our kisses, our passion as vaporous
as our breath in the air. At the family cottage

each weekend, her parents leave us more alone.
We cannot see if we are betraying their trust
or fulfilling their weary expectations. They fall
asleep as the snow drifts high against the cabin.

A black and white television buzzes down
on our fumbling ardor. Buttons fall open
and zippers smile and all that we carry here
is released into each other, into the white.

The Made Bed

I came to parenting early and by accident.
Thrashing from youth's soil, roots exposed,
adulthood bursting on me like a newborn's
first light of day, I starched my shirt

and tied my tie and pulled on the sober wool
suit of fatherhood. We drove 51 South all day
and the child played in the backseat playpen
carpentered by his grandfather. He cooed and giggled

and lavished over-the-seat hugs on his parents.
Late that night, in a small roadside motel, he cried,
no, screamed, at the loss of routine, the strange
bed, the estrangement from grandparents

who had overseen his molecule-by-molecule
manifest. He screamed and then, for the first time,
all anger and sorrow, I spanked the child. His mother,
for the first time, intervened and I left, crashing

the hollow wooden door against its metal frame.
Outside, I paced the meager dimensions of the gray
gravel parking lot, threw rocks, smoked cheap,
flavored cigarillos. Daylight still hours away,

I checked the room; the crying had ceased.
Carefully, I crept in, saw the child asleep in her arms.
Afraid to disturb the restive slumber, I settled
into the cracked vinyl embrace of a side chair.

Curtains filtered the fluorescent and neon waves
illuminating the jagged tableau: mother and child,
bed and chair, scattered clothes and toys, an open suitcase,
and me, constructor of labyrinths.

Swept Away by a
Confluence of Events

Events reside on lines, vectors of one
slope or another, their momentum
corresponding to their specific
inclination and their bond with the laws
of inertia and entropy. Like a long,
gypsy train, history as we know it
accumulates, measures, uses, and discards
its component vectors, its lines inexorably
converging like those in elementary
perspective. Poised at the event horizon,
heedless to the certainty of oblivion and the flat
blackness of our destiny, we recalculate
the coordinates, order another round,
sing one more verse, hoist our glasses
to our old friend gravity
and its ethereal cousin, free will.

Dee, 1922–1974

Sister loved uniforms, married a soldier
in Paris, Texas, during the war. From somewhere
in Europe, he wrote her letters, one on a silk
scarf fashioned into a parachute. She danced

with the airmen from Walnut Ridge, withstood
parental disdain, danced anyway. After
the divorce, she moved to Little Rock, worked
for the phone company, then for Sears, downtown

—neon animation, electrified buses, 1948.
She followed cousins and uncles west
to California, discovered the ocean and a sailor.
She brought him home, married him

in our working-class Missionary Baptist church.
They drove back west, settled in La Jolla.
She watched her sailor go to sea, waited,
then moved back home. He followed;

they fought. They separated, divorced fifteen
years later. Even then she felt betrayed, cried,
demanded recompense. She lived with Mother,
always with Mother, changed doctors, diseases,

drugs, but not druggists. She died one summer
solstice, victim of a hospital heart attack born
of a coughing spasm induced by the narcissus
stuffed casually in the orderly's uniform pocket.

Jay's Lounge and Cockpit, 1979

We tumble into the coldest room in Louisiana.
Wind dances through the walls
and two-steps through the gumbo
crowd. Everyone knows everyone except us.

Jukebox perfume, no band yet. We keep our coats on,
keep moving, laughing, talking: we belong.
Across a breezeway, through a pair of doors,
another room, a gas-burning space heater,

no music, but even more people, milling about
a miniature arena. Men are bragging, gesturing,
laughing and showing their tobacco-brown teeth.
Something seethes in the vented cases carried

into this room under proud, protective arms,
something alive and mad. Old blood stains
the concrete floor; money sprouts from fists.
Mercifully, the drum kicks, heels click on the floor

and the beat pulls us back across the breezy divide
where we huddle together near the bandstand,
watch Clifton and Cleveland draw their hands across keyboard
and rubboard, squeezing life back into this zydeco night.

Afloat in the Florida Parishes

On the Tangipahoa, we tube downstream
on a sunburning July weekend. We are mid-run,
mid-day, soon to be stopping for lunch
and switching from cola to beer.

There are eleven of us. I am in the center
of three tubes: an ice chest on my right
and my six-year-old son on the left.
In the shallows, he darts away to play,

comes splashing back as the water rushes,
grows deeper. We coast around a bend to find
a tangle of tree limbs blocking the right passage.
The first nine push and maneuver their way

around, but Ryan, the ice chest, and I are caught.
I cling to a slippery, gnarly limb and try to free us.
I turn to tell Ryan to hold tight just in time
to see him slide out of the tube, under the jam,

watch him disappear in the brown water. His mother
screams, dives. I hold the limb and crash my head
into the swirling water, groping for evidence
of flesh or bone. Up for air, I see blank faces,

then, a hundred feet downstream a blond head
and young, flailing arms fighting for safe passage.
A stranger fishes him out, delivers him to his mother's
hungry arms. Impatiently, I clear the jam and join

the others on the opposite shore. We take longer
than usual for lunch. Little is said as we move
back into the river for the journey's conclusion.
We never talk about it; we never go back.

My Romantic Legerdemain

Who are these women, and why do they spread
such vicious truths? I speak only for myself,
and even that may imply too firm a judgment.

Wife after suburban wife tumbles in liquid
disarray, framing the blank release of breath, the desire
to live out each plot, inhabit each house and life,

but lightly. Into this rises love, random and existential,
reliant upon a chance complicity of coordinates
and my own unquiet heart. Karen told me,

one toxic night when I was melancholy,
you must learn to be aloof, don't let them see,
don't let them know your needs

or even that you have them. Ellen said go
find the grownups and play with them; she told me
stories about lives I could have known. Sometimes

I live in a field of stars, novae in bloom, a cascade
of sixteenth notes punching through the clueless
sky, but when I rest, the women inside begin

again, talking about a certain quickness of hand,
about time without nostalgia, numbers greater
than one, a life outside parentheses.

Melinda's Sable

I never inquired about its origins,
so I can't account for the correctness
of her politics. I know that she used it
not for warmth or glamour,
but for drama, the sweep of December fur
crowned by her July hair.

She made glowing exits from cars,
a long splash of leg as the overture
for the grand and practiced event.

She paused at the entrance of rooms
like a quarterback
checking out the defense.

Her closest friend was bound for surgery,
the outcome uncertain. He was older,
more uncle than friend, his lust for her
a shared and abiding joke.

She was there in the morning
while the attendants prepared him.
As they carted him to O.R., she stood behind,
caught his eye and slowly opened the coat.

The surgeon said that he smiled as he went under.
The same smile greeted her in recovery, where
he testified at great length on the healing powers
of fur and skin.

Marcel on Fire

In the Garden District, the waiter deals two martinis,
Dubonnet, absinthe, and a glass of very dry chablis;
we fan the menus, absorbed in the glittering details.

Charles takes command of the wine list with the same
concentration he brought to the political coup
we celebrate tonight. Barbara's eyes trace

the live oak limbs through the garden window.
Our consultant, Bob, proposes a toast to our families,
our futures, our health. The second martini revives Dick,

who has suddenly assumed the personality
of some dead black guitar hero. Each course lingers
as our conversation rises and falls. It is raining

in the garden as dessert arrives, flaming.
Dick names the waiter "Marcel," and proposes
that he mount the table and ignite himself for our pleasure.

Gathering Evening

Late Friday afternoon, late spring, delta
macadam curves and trots like a precocious colt
through newly planted fields. Cardinals flash
in my car's path, daredevils of the highway

stirring a quarter-century-old memory,
a dead redbird in the sixty Chevy grill.
Black folk wave at the passing stranger. Mer Rouge
has a new water tower and an old

Dairy Hub and Saturday night is still
Saturday night. Now the darkness and light
are evening; now consider the chances.
Was it the smell of loam and fertilizer?

Was it something that escaped through the rafters
of the Jerusalem Baptist Church in a land
of crossroads, legends, voodoo, souls for rent?
A few decades back, one geological

summer, two professors walked this land
and saw through the cracks of the evening
what no one else could see: that they were walking,
no, not on a hill, not on a bluff,

but on a monument overgrown with crops,
trees, and forgetfulness, gouged by the tilling
blades, poisoned weekly by the yellow hot rod
with wings parked next to a tin building a couple

miles back. Ton after ton of earth carefully
arranged in Bronze Age harmonics, a thunderbird
rediscovered after all these Bayou Maçon years:
clay balls and pottery shards, bones, bones.

Mercury Rising

The rearview mirror hovers, explodes
over my shoulder with the light of the sun,
captures and reflects back to me the memory

of my desperate drives, the last unarmed man
in America, on the road and restless, approaching
the day as if I have just been slapped into life.

I flip the sideview skyward and scan for choppers,
rotate it until I am satisfied that there are no witnesses
to my despondent incantations.

I always thought that I would die in a library,
in the corner by the magazines, felled by a curious
disease, hollow as the men of modernity.

Instead, I live with the knowledge, the aching trace
of a lifetime arcing across the harvest of years
barely noticed in their season but regarded

with regret as each grows smaller, harder
to catch in the rearview. The sidereal knowledge
that the brandy-colored past makes fools

of otherwise intelligent men, and night
is the welcome stirring of angels
who notify the next of kin.

A Six-Pack and a Long Fuse

On his car phone, he calls at nine o'clock,
says he has a six-pack of Dos Equis
and does not want to drink alone. A few minutes
later I open my kitchen door to the beer

and a bear hug. He says he knew my wife
was out of town and thought I could use
the company. I turn on the stereo, play
it loud until after two. We do not talk

about my wayward son, or his apocalyptic
threats, or the privileged conversations
the two of them have had of late.
As I maneuver him out of the den and

toward the door, the words lodged
in his throat these past few hours spill
into the kitchen. "My father," he says,
"killed himself when I was nine."

Receding Attractions

He will tell you that he has seen them
self-combust, flames in the hallway,
down to ashes before therapists or lawyers
could be summoned. He has watched
mystified friends sifting the debris for clues,
aching for evidence of a co-respondent arsonist,
a fall guy or a fallen woman.

Others he has seen drain kindling dry
over time, seen them take precautions,
install sprinklers and smoke alarms.
Some continued for decades, only to be
swept away by the first random spark
from a late August thunderstorm.

His own flashed and fumed, turned in false
alarms for the thrill of the approaching siren.
At times it smoldered like old newspapers
in a dream basement. The flames previewed
at a cinema near his own neighborhood.
Without heroes or villains to yell "Fire!"

the end came, but there were no flashing
lights, no firehoses snaking down the street.
The change was just a ripple
under freshly laundered sheets,
two bodies in the slow-motion thrall
of love's bloodless retreat.

Paper Cut

Odd to be constrained this way
by the dimensions of the paper,
not the inches and millimeters
across and down,
but by the flatness,
the baleful twoness of dimension.

Desire would dance these words around,
spin them through measured space
like an architect,
with verses soaring to connect
weight-bearing columns
and, with Escherlike precision,
angle against the grain of logic,
turning down while glancing up,
to see a universe briefly revealed:
an origami amoeba strip,
dreaming while believing
while persisting in a memory,
this reason to deceive.

Passion's Sextant

You burn like Apollo
when our orbits
intersect and passion flares;

then you circle to a secret place,
a safer constellation,
orbiting an older sun,

a previous destination.
You put light years between us;
I wait without patience.

We navigate without instruments,
triangulate in search
of a common event.

We escape gravity's sadness
perform parallel turns
and face the madness,

the long black fall
of comet fragments
into the gas giant.

Our hearts beat wildly,
confronting the terror
of intimate knowledge.

Particle Storm

Over lunch today I told a friend about you.
I rambled on, paused in reverie, rambled more,
describing the different women I find in you.

I talked about your face, with and without
makeup. How your DNA mutates with each change
of clothes, how you feel with your whole heart.

I described your vapor trails, our passion's geometry,
a rainbow in a hailstorm. I told him how we sat
in my car for hours on a rainy Saturday afternoon

in an empty parking lot, the windows closed
with fog. I tried to paste the pieces together,
to arrange them into a mosaic resembling the full

portrait of you that I carry in my heart. I told him
how I know each of the women that you are;
but I could not assemble you from the pieces.

My friend smiled at seeing me so extravagantly
at sea, your pointillist image storming around me,
synapses dusting the afternoon sun.

Deconstructing Certainty

You tell me that it is not your nature to miss
someone. I serve up reason but it flies past you,
curls out of the window and circles Dali's pocketwatch,
there draped across the limb of the crape myrtle.

I retreat, take refuge in the pictures at this exhibition,
collected by a dead robber baron playing benefactor
in his afterlife. I move from cluster to cluster,
squinting to read the placards, some of which explain

the lowered lighting. Midway through the impressionists
I can feel the canon of Western art crumble
before a rumbling samba of greater and lesser
truths. A ragtag band of out-of-school painters

finagle a ride on some crazy breeze, set off
to reexamine the relationships between brushes
and strokes, light and space, viewer and object.
Meanwhile, in the cloisters, where the only wind

is mechanical, the dean of the art school poses
with his postmodern beer, wonders if analysis
is ever enough. I reassemble in the gift shop,
buy a card designed to make you miss me.

A Separate Vacation

A raft of pelicans in formation
banks like a squadron of bombers,
wings synchronized a scant twenty feet
above the ground. Vector established,
they cruise the shoreline,
aloof observers of the politics of beaches.

The wet sand is compressed into a hard surface
and above this, just an inch above,
there are microbursts of airborne grit
sweeping down the beach in waves,
like leaves dancing to autumn sonatas.
The wind is constant, east to west.

Back in the condo, I punch in your number,
listen to the rings, the clicks, the recorded message,
then add my hangup to the collection.
I turn on the television, inventory
the soaps and games, flip past Oprah
and Phil, consign the screen to darkness.

At midnight, I walk against the wind,
greet the occasional handholding couple.
From a party down the beach, I hear the insistent
ebb and ascent of island music. Alone in the dunes,
I rest, awash in voices bearing laughter, the warm
embrace of bourbon, the sweet fire of oblivion.

Black Wool,
Red Satin Lining

I wrote a moving speech
intended to make you cry,
to change your mind.
I delivered it with wounded eyes,
but you pulled the night around you
like a cape. I lost you in its folds,
and when I called
there was no answer.

I heard them play your song last night.
Searching the crowd for a dancer,
I asked an empty chair: it turned me down.
You were following your headlights,
crying over missing things.
I boarded the late-night blur:
last call, pay phone, wrong number,
no answer.

I set the speech to music but failed
to account for the broken strings,
the lacquered truths. No one hummed
the shadowy refrain or mouthed
the disappointing rhymes.
My arms no substitute for answers
and lovers left behind, you pulled
the night around you like a cape.

The Seventh Movement

A hot air balloon the color of a turnip,
My bloody friend the moon was full and rising
Through a curtain of storm clouds just above the trees.
I held you for hours as you lay across the front seat,
Head in my lap, at war with tears.

A nine-piece band with heads talking, rapid eye
Movement, a one-man horn section cheating
On accordion, subtropical percussion, and some
Dancing gypsy woman on a wired fiddle.
The long ride home you lay across the front seat,
Head in my lap, at war with sleep.

Now I sit alone and rage begins its fiery trek
Through my nervous, overloaded system,
Victim of sentience brownout. Fuses blown,
We sacrifice our love on an altar of reason.
We abstain from feeling in the name of prudence.
I have tucked away the passion that drove me:
I can't feel it
I can't feel it
I can't feel it
Through the distance.

I do not wish to take turns with your love,
To watch you return and leave, day upon day,
But the distance does its job, freezes me with vertigo.
The distance shortens my breath and prolongs
Each anxious second; it does exactly as you ask
And maintains
The reluctant
Status
Quo.

A Schedule of Trains

after James Dickey

"We have all been in rooms we cannot die in,"
you read, accusing me of keeping
secrets safe in the specious
mystique I have invented for your pleasure.

Your defiance and independence established,
you wear a more passive mask,
now properly dazzled by my decadence.

Tonight, though, I will sit in solitary
dread, that when the emerald dust
sprinkled around our coupling settles,
when your fever cools,

love will be a curious and distant malady,
tolerated only as a drunken illusion
for the sake of art,
for the season's folly.

You will quit my bed
and my apartment, wisely, wisely.

That which remains
will consider your photograph,
your studied leave,
and whether this room,
once witness to the end of these comings and goings,
can ever be lived in again.

The End of Us

Last night I could see it, if only by indirection,
a trick of the light and the unfocused eye.
Unacknowledged, it lay at the edge of our practiced
routine, an artifact of our waning passion.

When you had gone, I knew it for the thing
that it will become, the redolent remainder
of charcoal and pollen in a subdivision spring.
You will not say it, wanting the blame to reside

elsewhere, preferably in the safety of neutral
events. I will not speak it, not tonight, not yet.
Exit wound and elegy, it may only be spoken
posthumously. Tonight it waits in my bed:

I will rest against its weight, turn it over
like an endgame with Bergman, like solitaire
in the waiting room, turn it over and over
until it turns up missing.

Time's Other Country

after William Stafford

When I return this time, most of them are gone.
I drive past their houses, dial their numbers,
but speak mostly to strangers. Those that I do find
are ghosts, evanescent and uneasy in my company.

Still, the scent of vanilla and columbine, the maple
and sumac, the cobalt sky drive me back
into the storm of events, the axis upon which
my life turned decades ago. I stop at a junior high

that was once a high school, walk the hallways
where custodians, like gnomes, skitter into hidden
passages. I sit in the stadium and let the torrent
of things lost rain down on me, one last time. I resume

my search at the library, but the city directory reveals
nothing. I cross the Eau Claire River bridge and turn
north onto old 51. An hour later, I exit
into lake country where my feelings rise up before me

like a dream of life before the fall. Near Goodnow,
a doe and two fawns stare me down before retreating
into the woods. Like a teenager, I whip my car
over these worn, winding roads, through a canopy

of birch and pine, shadow and light. By the time I see
the cottage on Birch Lake, I no longer need to stop.
Somewhere above Minocqua, I take a breath
without pain. There it is again: take it.

Cover Story

He launches his campaign
as a hate-seeking missile;
it glows nuclear with a treachery
that feeds on itself.
America loves this boy,
but the party regulars hate him,

fear him even more.
They all fall down,
careening to the right.
While they prattle, he dreams
of climbing that hill, joining that club:
the long hallways,
the longer knives.

Alfred E. Newman with a lapel flag,
combat boots, plenty of moxie,
his face peeks over the horizon
like the first scream in an American
serial killer love story.

Anna and the Rainbow

You do it with color:
posters and catalogs, brushes and prisms.
The color holds all the meaning;
the color is the medium
through which the energy
flashes into your spirit,
clearing the way for the morning's revelation.

With rare insight or blind luck
the government gives you a grant
to pursue the psyche and the spectra.
Classes in the use of color
become kinetic windows; your students
become patients; your syllabus a mantra.

Now you surf the waves of probability,
casting over the next crash of events,
snagging a small piece of the future.
You examine it as if it were the work
of some cyberpunk artisan, a spun glass
sculpture of virtual reality. This you offer
to the names in your datebook:
the healing, the gift.

Ray's Farm, Late December

He spreads the hay in the corral
and I watch his hands, remembering
how they swallowed my best fastball,
gloveless, unflinching; how he held

each of my three sons as infants,
balanced on just one of those mammoth
palms. The bales explode under his
rake, releasing into the quartz air

the quick moist smells of last spring.
The horses' hooves crash against
the frozen ground. Ray curses the leader,
shoos them away while he works.

I kick idly at the hay and ask him
if he remembers his holy season
as my father's shadow, the year
he carried a Bible to church, believing

that any thing that held my father so
must be very near to the heart of things.
He leans on the rake, swabs his forehead
with his John Deere cap, and asks me

how old I am. I marvel at the non sequitur,
then utter a number that seems impossible.
He winces, half smiles, and resumes raking.
Yeah, he says, I remember.

What God Loves

God loves a melodrama, the bases loaded
with two outs in the ninth,
a cheerleader's mother consorting
with murderers, the atomic scientists' clock
lurching towards midnight.

Boy gets girl loses girl
gets sick gets girl loses
life, the kidnapped honor-roll student's
pale face plastered on milk cartons.

God loves a fall,
the fully earned vertiginous
humus-grabbing of the once mighty,
the desperate little collapses
of the artless, the mean.

God loves a joke
that no one gets, imaginary numbers
and equations without proofs,
the line between the heart and mind,
the slouching towards Bethlehem.

The angry fist.

Judgment.

Redemption.

The partridge taking wing, clearing
the cover of grain in the second before lead shot
rends feather and flesh, before the sound
can overtake the deed.

Historic Restaurant
To Be Demolished

Jayne writes that the Log Cabin will be razed,
but I am less affected than she would think.
There is, I suppose, some slight sentimental
attachment to the worn green plastic booths,

to dim neural slides of late-night conversation,
friends long since discarded. Neither the food
nor the service was distinguished, so its demise
provokes no regret, evokes no sense of loss.

Of course they're tearing it down; it's what they do,
the endlessly practical people of Wisconsin. They
know that a new freeway is better than an old barn,
a new Wal-Mart an improvement over an old restaurant

that wasn't much anyway. My own grief is tempered
by other, deeper regrets, like the burning, a decade
after graduation, of the gothic red brick palace that was
the Rothschild village hall. On Friday nights, its dark

wooden theater seats were arranged at the edges
of the dance floor. Fifteen cents got you into Canteen,
no bands, just a host of 45 RPM records. Bouquets
of blue and pink lights surrounded the hall, recondite

as whispers, the perfect pale candescence for the chemical
tremors of teenage love. Autumnal walks down dark
gravel roads ended with the mass of the building rising
up before me, the chest-pumping cold-start thrill

of walking into that room, the couples circling
the rectangular dance floor, the painful compassion
of small-town girls, the night's slow last dance,
its promise of transcendence: timpani and strings.

Claudia, the World

Her bright edges in spin, she fiercely defends
Beauty. She collects languages, painters
and paintings, poets, an occasional lover
if the season allows.

Such is the case with an old friend
in Germany, married, but these days,
who isn't? He says he will divorce
to marry her, but she laughs him off,

reminds him of life's imperfections,
of the choices each has made, will make.
When she turns melancholy, she cashes her last
traveler's check for a ticket to Thailand,

where friends keep her until the urge
to reconsider ebbs. Back in America, she designs
a new product line, conquers OSHA's latest
madness, and fashions vacant raw material

into objects of function and light. She prowls
Government Street for new art, badgers her friends
for contributions to bail out some wayward artist,
then returns to each an abstract portrait

of and to the benefactor. Mornings she carries
thick coffee, Rilke, and Erasmus to her backyard.
She inventories the flora, hugs her wet retriever,
remembers asylum: sand and mud, barges, the river.

Whose Cow Are You?

for Mark Strand and Sinead O'Connor

Bad cow, the cutline proclaims, and the beast
stares out of the newsprint past the police
and their drawn guns, right through the photographer
and the others who have cornered him
in downtown Augusta. Bad for escaping
the slaughterhouse and cantering around the city
charging at peace officers and their vehicles,
scattering garbage cans, trampling through
lawns and gardens. Bad for clearing the flat,
ingenuous, uncomprehending stare of the herd,
the stench, corral and gate. Bad cow for knowing,
in this silver nitrate moment, for knowing
and fighting the real enemy.

Quarter Morning

An early morning meeting, followed by breakfast
in the courtyard. By mid-morning I am packed
and leaving, the lower Quarter still a sleepy pastel.
Dirty t-shirt and baggy blue pants, he strides purposefully

down Chartres. His beard makes his age a question,
but I place him at thirty. In one hand, he holds a head
of cabbage; in the other, a large black felt-tipped marker.
Just before Esplanade he stops, stares longingly

at the freshly painted side wall of an apartment house.
Brandishing the marker like a rapier, he redefines
the wall with a pattern that might involve hearts,
could be initials; maybe it's nothing, maybe it's art.

He stands back and dots the air meaningfully with the marker,
resumes his morning stroll. At the corner he menaces
oncoming traffic with the marker, clutches the cabbage
protectively. A moment later, he disappears

into Faubourg Marigny. I have stopped my car
to the bewilderment of the now-honking traffic
behind me. Resisting the urge to get out and explain
the significance of the marker and the cabbage,

I pull onto Esplanade, onto Claiborne, onto I-10.
Another blue storm is sweeping in from the Cajun prairie,
bearing down on Pontchartrain. There are white birds
in the trees, marking my retreat: no epiphany, no relief.

My Nephew's Chair

At thirty-nine, with fifteen years of baldness
behind him, he notices the ebbing of premature
jokes. His second wife is pregnant with their
second child; the first was stillborn. His mother

nervously monitors the pregnancy. He gave
up his first wife and drinking, both cold turkey,
simultaneously; he feels no need to return to either.
He is Salesman of the Year and feels the onset

of adulthood, tardy, but with full gravitational
effects. When his parents arrive for dinner, he chases
the doberman into the back yard. He shakes
his father's hand, hugs and kisses his mother.

Without irony, he serves drinks, hands his father
a can of his favorite cheap beer. When his father
moves to a chair, he says, "No, Dad, over here.
That's my chair." His wife and mother gasp,

his father pauses. He meets his father's eyes,
noting the glare's diminished severity. Steadily,
he slides into his chair, waving the abashed
older man to an adjacent but lesser position.

1949 Silvertone Console

I promised to return for it decades ago,
but still it sits in my sister's garage, orphaned
since I left home. Once it was the center
of the known universe, but the mighty gold

and orange glow of its tubes stands cloistered
by years of feathery dust. The turntable's maroon
felt shows the base metal beneath, its ancient
gears are jammed, the speaker brittle and silent.

Abandoned by my brother and sisters
when they moved into their own adult worlds,
it opened before me like a kaleidoscope. Inside
the lower cabinet was a stack of records,

wax disks I would scratch and spin at amazing
speeds (three of them). I reveled in thirty
years of music: big band, western swing,
blues, and something Louis Jordan was playing

that Chuck Berry would turn into rock and roll.
I tried every bass and treble setting, bought
new records, smaller but with bigger holes
and bigger beats. In 1962, the turntable quit,

and the whole thing was replaced by a modern,
portable affair. No one knows what became of that,
but the Silvertone sits in my sister's garage,
a sentinel waiting for childhood's mottled reprise.

Forgiveness

Mardi Gras has folded into Lent,
and the stars have gone home.
What passed for charm in torchlight and revelry
turns out to be decay and burglar bars.

Sadness envelops the city like a slowly releasing
toxic visitor from the river's edge.
No knife is held to its big charity throat;
no gun trembles against its uptown temple.

Throwing off its arsenic staples as Easter passes,
the city renews its spirit. A heady spring bouquet mingles
with the pungent waste of the Quarter. New Orleans
may forget but it does not, on this earth, forgive.

The Gospel According to David, the Latter

They have come for me with words,
but I have words for them, things that only I
can reveal. They have come for me with guns,
but we have guns, too, and they will die

by the count of their miscalculations. They
have men who wear armor; I have men
who will inhale bullets, joyfully for the glory
of their savior, for me, oh Lord, for me.

They have played for us great music,
but we have music, too, seven trumpets
and seven angels to play for them. When
the angels sing, the music of my enemies

will not be heard. When the fifth angel
blows his trumpet, my enemies will
be set upon by a torment of scorpions,
by locusts the size of horses.

When my enemies attack, they will suffer
the brilliance of the seventh angel, witness
the breaking of the seventh seal, know the fury
of seven visions, drink the blood of seven bowls.

My enemies will know the beast; they have always
known. This time by fire, this time by fire,
an angel with the key to the abyss will descend,
and I will see my throne, the seat of new heaven,

the deliverer of new earth. That in me which is unclean
I will fling into the abyss; it shall be my final testimony.
My enemies will be singed by the fires of hell;
I come soon. I will come soon.

She Begins in Medias Res

As if this were an ongoing Sunday morning dialogue
and not the stranger standing at my table.

> If you love planes the way I do, they show this restored
> P-40 flying down to South America and there's a 737
> behind it, you know, a camera-chase plane and the 737
> is flying at top speed but that's so slow the P-40 can barely
> stay in the air. My husband, he was crew chief on a P-40,
> and he said they broke the sound barrier back during
> the war but there wasn't a sound barrier then so they
> didn't know what they had done, but the pilot described
> it, just like the other pilots did later, the rattle and loss
> of control, the silence on the other side.

She wears a light blue sweatsuit, has midlength gray hair
hanging in washboard falls. She wipes her nose with a tissue
and stuffs it up one sleeve. Her eyes are wired and she looks
right at me but I can't speak and she says:

> So many things happen, during the war, you know,
> I told him one day, I said, I'm going to get a tape recorder
> and just turn it on and let you talk, but he trained down
> at Biloxi and while he was down there this priest, see,
> an Italian who was living in New Orleans, he would come
> to Biloxi, and they got to be friends, my husband would
> take him fishing, so after basic training my husband
> ended up in Rome and one day he goes to mass
> at St. Peter's and sees the pope and they recognize
> each other cause it's this priest from New Orleans,
> and the priest says he's been saving every Tuesday
> for Americans but nobody shows up so my husband
> goes back to the base and he rousts out all his friends
> and every Tuesday they go to mass whether they're
> Catholic or not. So many things happen. They flew
> wherever they needed to for supplies, Africa,

45

China, wherever, and sometimes my husband would fly
along and one day they went to India and when
he told me about it I said you saw the Taj Mahal
didn't you and he said yeah, it was shiny, you know,
put down put down, but then he told me that this
sergeant took them to within spitting distance into
a dirt floor hut and there was a fifteen-year-old
boy and two younger girls and they're all bleeding
to death from syphilis and the sergeant said now
get the hell out of here and don't come back so that's
what they did but when the war was over you know
nobody really cared anymore, nobody really wanted
them to come back but somebody said that we were
the GI generation, going to school on the GI bill, then
building America and I never really thought about it
like that but I guess we did, so many things happen,
well, here he is.

I look around to see who he is, but she's halfway
out the door to an aging Yellow Cab and when I wish
her well, she can't hear me. She's already talking
to the taxi driver and I dive into my paper to avoid
all the latent coffeehouse curiosity.

A Pilgrim in the City of Dreams

I drive aimlessly through New Orleans streets,
trying to distill venom from pointless rage. Just past
sundown, vagrant lightning, but no rain. You need
a gun to feel safe on this night; Louisiana

is a state of siege. The governor and his friends
carve out their shares of our future addictions.
The bond commission celebrates another closing,
another investigation. The school board wagers

the only progress it has ever made on an all or less
than nothing bid to escape the judge's scrutiny.
I drive through the warehouse district, under
the bridge, and past the wharves on Tchoupitoulas.

I turn right on Jackson, where the houses retain
each calorie of the day's heat, sending their tenants
to front porches and front yards, to parking lots
and street corners. They mill about, talking about

the long day, talking about the governor, talking
about the purchase of blind relief, talking about
that white man behind locked car doors, jittery-eyed,
driving down this street where he don't belong.

I go left on St. Charles, heading uptown where wolfhounds
and rottweilers are tethered to white couples jogging
along the streetcar tracks. In the boulevard's sway
(barred windows, security system signs, razor wire),

I dive like a balsawood glider catching just enough air
for one more, lesser, loop. A cache in my chest
hemorrhages fear. The remaining light shows rollerblades,
a turning lane, a traveler's entropy in magnetic fields.

Another False Spring

My oldest sister died on the longest day of the year.
She had lived with our widowed mother, so the siblings
were concerned. Mother, however, received phone calls

which she mysteriously took in the bedroom. We followed
and stood outside her door in vain: she spoke
so softly. A few days after the funeral, Mother told us

of her suitor, the first in fifteen years of widowhood.
His calls were the balm that her surviving offspring
could never apply. There, in grief's desolation,

stirred the seed of redemption, a seventy-year-old's girlish
courtship. The ensuing weeks brought revelation:
the suitor was a childhood sweetheart, unknown to us all,

a secret of our mother's youth. More than fifty years
had passed since their last kiss. In six months they were
married; Mother moved to his north Arkansas farm.

Early mornings, he rode his chestnut mare to the far reaches
of the half-section, where he picked woodland iris
for his bride's mahogany table. She baked biscuits,

made gravy, and moved giddily into the role of new wife
to the retired pharmacist, banker, and farmer. He died,
a heart too full of life, after just two years. She moved

back to a small house in Little Rock,
where her immense grief sustained her
with the memory of this love at last requited.

Trust

He died today, my next-door neighbor
when I was a child on Rosetta Street.
He was like family, my parents said,
and they entrusted me to him.

My father worked long hours, so the neighbor
took me to the ball park and bought hot dogs,
popcorn, and snow cones. His office had a picnic;
I went with him as a surrogate son.

In the fall, I came home early from school
and watched the World Series with him,
just the two of us and the Dumont TV,
the Yankees and the Dodgers again.

Now he's dead, his stale Roi-tan cigar
crushed in a standing ashtray, and I must
snuff this lifelong enmity that marks me
sure as a fingerprint. I will extinguish

the anger and revenge, cast out the memories
of gabardine pants, the zipper in motion,
his fingers, his ashen, suffocating breath,
and all the sordid little scars he left in me.

Healing the King

Some wild morning when love's debris
no longer intrudes like the ghost of a severed arm,
when the upstairs bedroom window admits
gold freshets of light and the flirting chance
of a breeze, when the Bakelite radio
plays Jo Stafford and Little Willie John
and the sheets pool like sugar and the air holds
the memory of last night's thundershower,
some wild morning the sun awakens
an obscure and somnolent wrinkle in twin helices.
Anima quickens in Parsifal's shadow:
thrum and scend, plainsong and descant.
Five sexes mark the angel, a child in water
who becomes his own wife.

A Life in Blue

Dying since she was twenty, she always
arranged for others to place her needs first,
to shelter her, care for her, love her.
Her auburn hair curled against the tide of age.

For years, my visits home moved ever closer
to babysitting. She went from frailness to a cane,
from the cane to a walker, from the walker to bed,
as rheumatoid arthritis raged, twisting and reducing

the already diminutive frame, grotesquely distorting
her feeble digits. Still, she carried on, past seventy,
past eighty; she approached ninety with resignation
and amazement, her memory subject to power

failure, her vision an impressionist's garden.
She said that many times she wanted no more
than to lie in her bed without hurting. Once though,
she rose from the bed, arranged flowers in a vase.

She summoned me to the porch to inhale springtime.
She watched the birds, regaled me with their songs
until her favorite bluebird appeared, electric
against the greenery. She chuckled and said,

"That's me, Son. When I die I will be a bluebird;
I will sing in your backyard." This, then is my
inheritance, a bluebird alive with freedom and song,
her twisted limbs discarded for the shimmer of wings.

The Drummer's Accomplice

for William Collins and Jo Carol Pierce

She was acting on her savior's instructions,
staying right with the beat she found in church,
having deeply spiritual, profoundly rhythmic
sex with every boy wearing a fancy belt

buckle. I made friends with her low sources,
but not everyone has read everyone, so she said
to shine the light that you are given and stay
with your own assigned beat. She believed

in the power of angels drawn on jocund day
but could not find one blessed virgin
in all of West Texas, not in the window screen,
not in a tree, not behind the checkout counter.

Clean as a B-flat saxophone break, she fell
in love with a moving train, mourned its passing
after midnight in the swing in my backyard.
Then it was all a search for old boyfriends,

for epiphanies in a Bo Diddley beat, for something
cataclysmic every millennium or two, for rising
above without leaving behind the gladness
and her rich-haired morning child self.

The Ephebe's Way

A dwarfish protector of what she deemed canonical—
sweet Tess and naughty Henry Fielding—but not
my faux Joyce making no sense, words not found

in a proper dictionary, she pursed her lips at me,
waved me off to the library rather than suffer my beat,
rowdy obsessions. I gave her nothing.

It was years of dissipation, incohesive and lachrymose
lines, a prayer for the cerebral cortex, a ritual fusion
down and away, before I awoke to a windowpane

paisley shirt, a blackwalled yellow Mustang
and, oh jesus, its blonde driver, the healing
of every tendril connection to the whole. Still

later, the quicksilver-bright, concrete-smart evening
division instructor said I must see you after,
make an appointment! Who are you, why are you

in my class, how do you feel about *The Graduate?*
The scene dissolved: better jobs, cars, clothes.
I lurched like a pinball through decades. Decades.

The odd inebriant, the song that follows turned
from murk into shiver and shimmer, no Doppler-
shifting bells before the northbound train, its fretting

generator, the emergent darkness. I never knew
a home that wheatfields could not chase away. Milky
hours alone, butterfly snow on the rented shield,

and finally, eerily sober, chill of blue sky, a voice
to be feared swerved from shore and bay, smithy
of the heart forging an artifice: echo, wing.

THANK YOU

Harmon and Ione
Betty, Bailey, and Dee
Rende, Jay, and Ryan
Ralene
Larry and Trent
Catherine Fry and Les Phillabaum
Wilma, Mavis, Phyllis, and Momma Sears
Dennis, Angela, Rebecca, Melinda, Cathy, and Bailey II
Sweet Nancy
Sue Owen
Edward Hirsch, Jorie Graham, James Dickey, and Harold Bloom
Susan Loach, Rubye Brashears, Patsy Campbell, and Helen Gary
Lucia Cordell Getsi, M. Mark
Yellow Bay and Bread Loaf
Wings of Desire, The Seventh Seal, 8½
James Joyce
Ellen Gilchrist
Bruce, Bob, and Joni
Charles Roemer II
The Dubois Poetry Group
All My Friends, All of Them